WEEKLY & MONTHLY
Academic
2023-2024 PLANNER

_____

NAME

Personal Mission Statement

Top Tasks

MONTHLY

August

- [ ] ....
- [ ] ....
- [ ] ....
- [ ] ....
- [ ] ....

September

- [ ] ....
- [ ] ....
- [ ] ....
- [ ] ....
- [ ] ....

October

- [ ] ....
- [ ] ....
- [ ] ....
- [ ] ....
- [ ] ....

November

- [ ] ....
- [ ] ....
- [ ] ....
- [ ] ....
- [ ] ....

December

- [ ] ....
- [ ] ....
- [ ] ....
- [ ] ....
- [ ] ....

January

- [ ] ....
- [ ] ....
- [ ] ....
- [ ] ....
- [ ] ....

February

- [ ] ....
- [ ] ....
- [ ] ....
- [ ] ....
- [ ] ....

March

- [ ] ....
- [ ] ....
- [ ] ....
- [ ] ....
- [ ] ....

April

- [ ] ....
- [ ] ....
- [ ] ....
- [ ] ....
- [ ] ....

May

- [ ] ....
- [ ] ....
- [ ] ....
- [ ] ....

June

- [ ] ....
- [ ] ....
- [ ] ....
- [ ] ....
- [ ] ....

July

- [ ] ....
- [ ] ....
- [ ] ....
- [ ] ....

Year

August

S	M	T	W	T	F	S
		1	2	3	4	5
6	7	8	9	10	11	12
13	14	15	16	17	18	19
20	21	22	23	24	25	26
27	28	29	30	31		

September

S	M	T	W	T	F	S
					1	2
3	4	5	6	7	8	9
10	11	12	13	14	15	16
17	18	19	20	21	22	23
24	25	26	27	28	29	30

October

S	M	T	W	T	F	S
1	2	3	4	5	6	7
8	9	10	11	12	13	14
15	16	17	18	19	20	21
22	23	24	25	26	27	28
29	30	31				

November

S	M	T	W	T	F	S
			1	2	3	4
5	6	7	8	9	10	11
12	13	14	15	16	17	18
19	20	21	22	23	24	25
26	27	28	29	30		

December

S	M	T	W	T	F	S
					1	2
3	4	5	6	7	8	9
10	11	12	13	14	15	16
17	18	19	20	21	22	23
24	25	26	27	28	29	30
31						

January

S	M	T	W	T	F	S
	1	2	3	4	5	6
7	8	9	10	11	12	13
14	15	16	17	18	19	20
21	22	23	24	25	26	27
28	29	30	31			

February

S	M	T	W	T	F	S
				1	2	3
4	5	6	7	8	9	10
11	12	13	14	15	16	17
18	19	20	21	22	23	24
25	26	27	28	29		

March

S	M	T	W	T	F	S
					1	2
3	4	5	6	7	8	9
10	11	12	13	14	15	16
17	18	19	20	21	22	23
24	25	26	27	28	29	30
31						

April

S	M	T	W	T	F	S
	1	2	3	4	5	6
7	8	9	10	11	12	13
14	15	16	17	18	19	20
21	22	23	24	25	26	27
28	29	30				

May

S	M	T	W	T	F	S
			1	2	3	4
5	6	7	8	9	10	11
12	13	14	15	16	17	18
19	20	21	22	23	24	25
26	27	28	29	30	31	

June

S	M	T	W	T	F	S
						1
2	3	4	5	6	7	8
9	10	11	12	13	14	15
16	17	18	19	20	21	22
23	24	25	26	27	28	29
30						

July

S	M	T	W	T	F	S
	1	2	3	4	5	6
7	8	9	10	11	12	13
14	15	16	17	18	19	20
21	22	23	24	25	26	27
28	29	30	31			

Notes
DATES, CONTACTS

Goal
PLANNING

August 2023

SUNDAY	MONDAY	TUESDAY	WEDNESDAY
		1	2
6	7	8	9
13	14	15	16
20	21	22	23
27	28	29	30

THURSDAY	FRIDAY	SATURDAY	Notes
3	4	5	
10	11	12	
17	18	19	
24	25	26	
31			

July 2023

30 Sunday	31 Monday	1 Tuesday	2 Wednesday
☐	☐	☐	☐
☐	☐	☐	☐
☐	☐	☐	☐

NOTES

3
Thursday

☐ ....
☐ ....
☐ ....
....
....
....
....
....
....
....
....
....
....
....
....
....
....
....
....

4
Friday

☐ ....
☐ ....
☐ ....
....
....
....
....
....
....
....
....
....
....
....
....
....
....
....
....

5
Saturday

☐ ....
☐ ....
☐ ....
....
....
....
....
....
....
....
....
....
....
....
....
....
....
....
....

TOP TASKS

☐ ....
☐ ....
☐ ....
☐ ....
☐ ....
☐ ....
☐ ....
☐ ....
☐ ....
☐ ....
☐ ....
☐ ....
☐ ....
☐ ....
☐ ....
☐ ....
☐ ....
☐ ....
☐ ....
☐ ....
☐ ....

NOTES

August 2023

6 Sunday	7 Monday	8 Tuesday	9 Wednesday
☐	☐	☐	☐
☐	☐	☐	☐
☐	☐	☐	☐

NOTES

10
Thursday

☐
☐
☐

11
Friday

☐
☐
☐

12
Saturday

☐
☐
☐

TOP TASKS

☐
☐
☐
☐
☐
☐
☐
☐
☐
☐
☐
☐
☐
☐
☐
☐
☐
☐
☐
☐

NOTES

August 2023

13 Sunday	14 Monday	15 Tuesday	16 Wednesday
☐	☐	☐	☐
☐	☐	☐	☐
☐	☐	☐	☐

NOTES

17
Thursday

☐ ....
☐ ....
☐ ....

18
Friday

☐ ....
☐ ....
☐ ....

19
Saturday

☐ ....
☐ ....
☐ ....

TOP TASKS

☐ ....
☐ ....
☐ ....
☐ ....
☐ ....
☐ ....
☐ ....
☐ ....
☐ ....
☐ ....
☐ ....
☐ ....
☐ ....
☐ ....
☐ ....
☐ ....
☐ ....
☐ ....
☐ ....
☐ ....

NOTES

20	21	22	23
Sunday	Monday	Tuesday	Wednesday

NOTES

24
Thursday

- ☐ ....
- ☐ ....
- ☐ ....

25
Friday

- ☐ ....
- ☐ ....
- ☐ ....

26
Saturday

- ☐ ....
- ☐ ....
- ☐ ....

TOP TASKS

- ☐ ....
- ☐ ....
- ☐ ....
- ☐ ....
- ☐ ....
- ☐ ....
- ☐ ....
- ☐ ....
- ☐ ....
- ☐ ....
- ☐ ....
- ☐ ....
- ☐ ....
- ☐ ....
- ☐ ....
- ☐ ....
- ☐ ....
- ☐ ....
- ☐ ....
- ☐ ....
- ☐ ....
- ☐ ....

NOTES

September 2023

SUNDAY	MONDAY	TUESDAY	WEDNESDAY
3	4	5	6
10	11	12	13
17	18	19	20
24	25	26	27

THURSDAY	FRIDAY	SATURDAY	Notes
	1	2	....
			....
			....
			....
7	8	9	....
			....
			....
14	15	16	....
			....
			....
21	22	23	....
			....
			....
28	29	30	....

August 2023

27 Sunday

- ☐ ....
- ☐ ....
- ☐ ....

28 Monday

- ☐ ....
- ☐ ....
- ☐ ....

29 Tuesday

- ☐ ....
- ☐ ....
- ☐ ....

30 Wednesday

- ☐ ....
- ☐ ....
- ☐ ....

NOTES

31 Thursday	1 Friday	2 Saturday	TOP TASKS
☐	☐	☐	☐
☐	☐	☐	☐
☐	☐	☐	☐
			☐
			☐
			☐
			☐
			☐
			☐
			☐
			☐
			☐
			☐
			☐
			☐
			☐
			☐
			☐
			☐
			☐

NOTES

September 2023

3 Sunday	4 Monday	5 Tuesday	6 Wednesday
☐	☐	☐	☐
☐	☐	☐	☐
☐	☐	☐	☐

NOTES

7
Thursday

☐ ....
☐ ....
☐ ....

8
Friday

☐ ....
☐ ....
☐ ....

9
Saturday

☐ ....
☐ ....
☐ ....

TOP TASKS

☐ ....
☐ ....
☐ ....
☐ ....
☐ ....
☐ ....
☐ ....
☐ ....
☐ ....
☐ ....
☐ ....
☐ ....
☐ ....
☐ ....
☐ ....
☐ ....
☐ ....
☐ ....
☐ ....
☐ ....
☐ ....

NOTES

September 2023

10 Sunday	11 Monday	12 Tuesday	13 Wednesday
☐	☐	☐	☐
☐	☐	☐	☐
☐	☐	☐	☐

NOTES

September 2023

14 Thursday	15 Friday	16 Saturday	TOP TASKS
☐	☐	☐	☐
☐	☐	☐	☐
☐	☐	☐	☐
			☐
			☐
			☐
			☐
			☐
			☐
			☐
			☐
			☐
			☐
			☐
			☐
			☐
			☐
			☐
			☐
			☐

NOTES

September 2023

17	18	19	20
Sunday	Monday	Tuesday	Wednesday

17 Sunday
- ☐ ....
- ☐ ....
- ☐ ....

18 Monday
- ☐ ....
- ☐ ....
- ☐ ....

19 Tuesday
- ☐ ....
- ☐ ....
- ☐ ....

20 Wednesday
- ☐ ....
- ☐ ....
- ☐ ....

NOTES

21 Thursday	22 Friday	23 Saturday	TOP TASKS
☐	☐	☐	☐
☐	☐	☐	☐
☐	☐	☐	☐
			☐
			☐
			☐
			☐
			☐
			☐
			☐
			☐
			☐
			☐
			☐
			☐
			☐
			☐
			☐
			☐
			☐

OTES

September 2023

24 Sunday	25 Monday	26 Tuesday	27 Wednesday
☐	☐	☐	☐
☐	☐	☐	☐
☐	☐	☐	☐

NOTES

28 Thursday	29 Friday	30 Saturday	TOP TASKS
☐	☐	☐	☐
☐	☐	☐	☐
☐	☐	☐	☐
			☐
			☐
			☐
			☐
			☐
			☐
			☐
			☐
			☐
			☐
			☐
			☐
			☐
			☐
			☐
			☐
			☐

NOTES

October 2023

SUNDAY	MONDAY	TUESDAY	WEDNESDAY
1	2	3	4
8	9	10	11
15	16	17	18
22	23	24	25
29	30	31	

THURSDAY	FRIDAY	SATURDAY	Notes
5	6	7	....
12	13	14	....
19	20	21	....
26	27	28	....
			....

October 2023

1 Sunday	2 Monday	3 Tuesday	4 Wednesday
☐	☐	☐	☐
☐	☐	☐	☐
☐	☐	☐	☐

NOTES

5
Thursday

- [ ]
- [ ]
- [ ]

6
Friday

- [ ]
- [ ]
- [ ]

7
Saturday

- [ ]
- [ ]
- [ ]

TOP TASKS

- [ ]
- [ ]
- [ ]
- [ ]
- [ ]
- [ ]
- [ ]
- [ ]
- [ ]
- [ ]
- [ ]
- [ ]
- [ ]
- [ ]
- [ ]
- [ ]
- [ ]
- [ ]
- [ ]
- [ ]

NOTES

October 2023

8 Sunday	9 Monday	10 Tuesday	11 Wednesday
☐	☐	☐	☐
☐	☐	☐	☐
☐	☐	☐	☐

NOTES

12
Thursday

☐ ....
☐ ....
☐ ....

13
Friday

☐ ....
☐ ....
☐ ....

14
Saturday

☐ ....
☐ ....
☐ ....

TOP TASKS

☐ ....
☐ ....
☐ ....
☐ ....
☐ ....
☐ ....
☐ ....
☐ ....
☐ ....
☐ ....
☐ ....
☐ ....
☐ ....
☐ ....
☐ ....
☐ ....
☐ ....
☐ ....
☐ ....
☐ ....

NOTES

15
Sunday

☐ ....
☐ ....
☐ ....

16
Monday

☐ ....
☐ ....
☐ ....

17
Tuesday

☐ ....
☐ ....
☐ ....

18
Wednesday

☐ ....
☐ ....
☐ ....

NOTES

19 Thursday	20 Friday	21 Saturday	TOP TASKS
☐	☐	☐	☐
☐	☐	☐	☐
☐	☐	☐	☐
			☐
			☐
			☐
			☐
			☐
			☐
			☐
			☐
			☐
			☐
			☐
			☐
			☐
			☐
			☐
			☐
			☐

OTES

October 2023

22 Sunday	23 Monday	24 Tuesday	25 Wednesday
☐	☐	☐	☐
☐	☐	☐	☐
☐	☐	☐	☐

NOTES

26
Thursday

☐
☐
☐

27
Friday

☐
☐
☐

28
Saturday

☐
☐
☐

TOP TASKS

☐
☐
☐
☐
☐
☐
☐
☐
☐
☐
☐
☐
☐
☐
☐
☐
☐
☐
☐
☐
☐

NOTES

November 2023

SUNDAY	MONDAY	TUESDAY	WEDNESDAY
			1
5	6	7	8
12	13	14	15
19	20	21	22
26	27	28	29

THURSDAY	FRIDAY	SATURDAY	Notes
2	3	4	
9	10	11	
16	17	18	
23	24	25	
30			

October 2023

29 Sunday	30 Monday	31 Tuesday	1 Wednesday
☐	☐	☐	☐
☐	☐	☐	☐
☐	☐	☐	☐

NOTES

2
Thursday

- ☐ ....
- ☐ ....
- ☐ ....

3
Friday

- ☐ ....
- ☐ ....
- ☐ ....

4
Saturday

- ☐ ....
- ☐ ....
- ☐ ....

TOP TASKS

- ☐
- ☐
- ☐
- ☐
- ☐
- ☐
- ☐
- ☐
- ☐
- ☐
- ☐
- ☐
- ☐
- ☐
- ☐
- ☐
- ☐
- ☐
- ☐

NOTES

November 2023

5 Sunday	6 Monday	7 Tuesday	8 Wednesday
☐	☐	☐	☐
☐	☐	☐	☐
☐	☐	☐	☐

NOTES

9 Thursday	10 Friday	11 Saturday	TOP TASKS
☐ ··········	☐ ··········	☐ ··········	☐ ··········
☐ ··········	☐ ··········	☐ ··········	☐ ··········
☐ ··········	☐ ··········	☐ ··········	☐ ··········
··········	··········	··········	☐ ··········
··········	··········	··········	☐ ··········
··········	··········	··········	☐ ··········
··········	··········	··········	☐ ··········
··········	··········	··········	☐ ··········
··········	··········	··········	☐ ··········
··········	··········	··········	☐ ··········
··········	··········	··········	☐ ··········
··········	··········	··········	☐ ··········
··········	··········	··········	☐ ··········
··········	··········	··········	☐ ··········
··········	··········	··········	☐ ··········
··········	··········	··········	☐ ··········
··········	··········	··········	☐ ··········
··········	··········	··········	☐ ··········
··········	··········	··········	☐ ··········
··········	··········	··········	☐ ··········
··········	··········	··········	☐ ··········

NOTES

November 2023

12 Sunday	13 Monday	14 Tuesday	15 Wednesday
☐	☐	☐	☐
☐	☐	☐	☐
☐	☐	☐	☐

NOTES

| 16 | 17 | 18 | TOP |
| Thursday | Friday | Saturday | TASKS |

☐ .... ☐ .... ☐ .... ☐ ....
☐ .... ☐ .... ☐ .... ☐ ....
☐ .... ☐ .... ☐ .... ☐ ....
☐ ....
☐ ....
☐ ....
☐ ....
☐ ....
☐ ....
☐ ....
☐ ....
☐ ....
☐ ....
☐ ....
☐ ....
☐ ....
☐ ....

OTES

November 2023

19 Sunday	20 Monday	21 Tuesday	22 Wednesday
☐	☐	☐	☐ ....
☐	☐	☐	☐ ....
☐	☐	☐	☐ ....

NOTES

23 Thursday	24 Friday	25 Saturday	TOP TASKS
☐	☐	☐	☐
☐	☐	☐	☐
☐	☐	☐	☐
			☐
			☐
			☐
			☐
			☐
			☐
			☐
			☐
			☐
			☐
			☐
			☐
			☐
			☐
			☐
			☐
			☐

OTES

December 2023

SUNDAY	MONDAY	TUESDAY	WEDNESDAY
3	4	5	6
10	11	12	13
17	18	19	20
24	25	26	27
31			

THURSDAY	FRIDAY	SATURDAY	Notes
	1	2	....
			....
7	8	9	....
			....
14	15	16	....
			....
21	22	23	....
			....
28	29	30	....

26 Sunday	27 Monday	28 Tuesday	29 Wednesday
☐	☐	☐	☐ ....
☐	☐	☐	☐ ....
☐	☐	☐	☐ ....

NOTES

30
Thursday

- [ ]
- [ ]
- [ ]

1
Friday

- [ ]
- [ ]
- [ ]

2
Saturday

- [ ]
- [ ]
- [ ]

TOP TASKS

- [ ]
- [ ]
- [ ]
- [ ]
- [ ]
- [ ]
- [ ]
- [ ]
- [ ]
- [ ]
- [ ]
- [ ]
- [ ]
- [ ]
- [ ]
- [ ]
- [ ]
- [ ]
- [ ]
- [ ]

NOTES

December 2023

3 Sunday	4 Monday	5 Tuesday	6 Wednesday
☐	☐	☐	☐
☐	☐	☐	☐
☐	☐	☐	☐

NOTES

7
Thursday

☐ ....
☐ ....
☐ ....

....
....
....
....
....
....
....
....
....
....
....
....
....
....
....
....
....

8
Friday

☐ ....
☐ ....
☐ ....

....
....
....
....
....
....
....
....
....
....
....
....
....
....
....
....
....

9
Saturday

☐ ....
☐ ....
☐ ....

....
....
....
....
....
....
....
....
....
....
....
....
....
....
....
....
....

TOP TASKS

☐ ....
☐ ....
☐ ....
☐ ....
☐ ....
☐ ....
☐ ....
☐ ....
☐ ....
☐ ....
☐ ....
☐ ....
☐ ....
☐ ....
☐ ....
☐ ....
☐ ....
☐ ....
☐ ....
☐ ....

NOTES

December 2023

10 Sunday	11 Monday	12 Tuesday	13 Wednesday
☐	☐	☐	☐
☐	☐	☐	☐
☐	☐	☐	☐

NOTES

14
Thursday

☐ ....
☐ ....
☐ ....

15
Friday

☐ ....
☐ ....
☐ ....

16
Saturday

☐ ....
☐ ....
☐ ....

TOP TASKS

☐ ....
☐ ....
☐ ....
☐ ....
☐ ....
☐ ....
☐ ....
☐ ....
☐ ....
☐ ....
☐ ....
☐ ....
☐ ....
☐ ....
☐ ....
☐ ....
☐ ....
☐ ....
☐ ....
☐ ....
☐ ....

NOTES

December 2023

17 Sunday	18 Monday	19 Tuesday	20 Wednesday
☐	☐	☐	☐
☐	☐	☐	☐
☐	☐	☐	☐

NOTES

21
Thursday

☐ ....
☐ ....
☐ ....

22
Friday

☐ ....
☐ ....
☐ ....

23
Saturday

☐ ....
☐ ....
☐ ....

TOP TASKS

☐ ....
☐ ....
☐ ....
☐ ....
☐ ....
☐ ....
☐ ....
☐ ....
☐ ....
☐ ....
☐ ....
☐ ....
☐ ....
☐ ....
☐ ....
☐ ....
☐ ....
☐ ....
☐ ....

NOTES

December 2023

24 Sunday	25 Monday	26 Tuesday	27 Wednesday
☐	☐	☐	☐
☐	☐	☐	☐
☐	☐	☐	☐

NOTES

28
Thursday

☐ ....
☐ ....
☐ ....
....
....
....
....
....
....
....
....
....
....
....
....
....

29
Friday

☐ ....
☐ ....
☐ ....
....
....
....
....
....
....
....
....
....
....
....
....
....

30
Saturday

☐ ....
☐ ....
☐ ....
....
....
....
....
....
....
....
....
....
....
....
....
....

TOP TASKS

☐ ....
☐ ....
☐ ....
☐ ....
☐ ....
☐ ....
☐ ....
☐ ....
☐ ....
☐ ....
☐ ....
☐ ....
☐ ....
☐ ....
☐ ....
☐ ....
☐ ....
☐ ....
☐ ....
☐ ....

NOTES

January 2024

SUNDAY	MONDAY	TUESDAY	WEDNESDAY
	1	2	3
7	8	9	10
14	15	16	17
21	22	23	24
28	29	30	31

THURSDAY	FRIDAY	SATURDAY	Notes
4	5	6	
11	12	13	
18	19	20	
25	26	27	

December 2023

31 Sunday	1 Monday	2 Tuesday	3 Wednesday
☐	☐	☐	☐
☐	☐	☐	☐
☐	☐	☐	☐

NOTES

4
Thursday

☐
☐
☐

5
Friday

☐
☐
☐

6
Saturday

☐
☐
☐

TOP TASKS

☐
☐
☐
☐
☐
☐
☐
☐
☐
☐
☐
☐
☐
☐
☐
☐
☐
☐
☐
☐

NOTES

January 2024

7 Sunday	8 Monday	9 Tuesday	10 Wednesday
☐	☐	☐	☐
☐	☐	☐	☐
☐	☐	☐	☐

NOTES

11
Thursday

- ☐ ....
- ☐ ....
- ☐ ....

12
Friday

- ☐ ....
- ☐ ....
- ☐ ....

13
Saturday

- ☐ ....
- ☐ ....
- ☐ ....

TOP TASKS

- ☐ ....
- ☐ ....
- ☐ ....
- ☐ ....
- ☐ ....
- ☐ ....
- ☐ ....
- ☐ ....
- ☐ ....
- ☐ ....
- ☐ ....
- ☐ ....
- ☐ ....
- ☐ ....
- ☐ ....
- ☐ ....
- ☐ ....
- ☐ ....
- ☐ ....
- ☐ ....

OTES

January 2024

14 Sunday	15 Monday	16 Tuesday	17 Wednesday
☐	☐	☐	☐
☐	☐	☐	☐
☐	☐	☐	☐

NOTES

18 Thursday	19 Friday	20 Saturday	TOP TASKS
☐	☐	☐	☐
☐	☐	☐	☐
☐	☐	☐	☐
			☐
			☐
			☐
			☐
			☐
			☐
			☐
			☐
			☐
			☐
			☐
			☐
			☐
			☐
			☐
			☐

NOTES

21 Sunday	22 Monday	23 Tuesday	24 Wednesday
☐	☐	☐	☐
☐	☐	☐	☐
☐	☐	☐	☐

NOTES

25 Thursday	26 Friday	27 Saturday	TOP TASKS
☐	☐	☐	☐
☐	☐	☐	☐
☐	☐	☐	☐
			☐
			☐
			☐
			☐
			☐
			☐
			☐
			☐
			☐
			☐
			☐
			☐
			☐
			☐
			☐
			☐
			☐

NOTES

February 2024

SUNDAY	MONDAY	TUESDAY	WEDNESDAY
4	5	6	7
11	12	13	14
18	19	20	21
25	26	27	28

THURSDAY	FRIDAY	SATURDAY	Notes
1	2	3	....
8	9	10	....
15	16	17	....
22	23	24	....
29			....

January 2024

28 Sunday	29 Monday	30 Tuesday	31 Wednesday
☐	☐	☐	☐
☐	☐	☐	☐
☐	☐	☐	☐

NOTES

1
Thursday

☐ ....
☐ ....
☐ ....

2
Friday

☐ ....
☐ ....
☐ ....

3
Saturday

☐ ....
☐ ....
☐ ....

TOP TASKS

☐ ....
☐ ....
☐ ....
☐ ....
☐ ....
☐ ....
☐ ....
☐ ....
☐ ....
☐ ....
☐ ....
☐ ....
☐ ....
☐ ....
☐ ....
☐ ....
☐ ....
☐ ....
☐ ....

NOTES

February 2024

4 Sunday	5 Monday	6 Tuesday	7 Wednesday
☐	☐	☐	☐
☐	☐	☐	☐
☐	☐	☐	☐

NOTES

8 Thursday	9 Friday	10 Saturday	TOP TASKS
☐	☐	☐	☐
☐	☐	☐	☐
☐	☐	☐	☐
			☐
			☐
			☐
			☐
			☐
			☐
			☐
			☐
			☐
			☐
			☐
			☐
			☐
			☐
			☐
			☐
			☐
			☐

NOTES

February 2024

11 Sunday	12 Monday	13 Tuesday	14 Wednesday
☐	☐	☐	☐
☐	☐	☐	☐
☐	☐	☐	☐

NOTES

15
Thursday

- ☐ ....
- ☐ ....
- ☐ ....

16
Friday

- ☐ ....
- ☐ ....
- ☐ ....

17
Saturday

- ☐ ....
- ☐ ....
- ☐ ....

TOP TASKS

- ☐
- ☐
- ☐
- ☐
- ☐
- ☐
- ☐
- ☐
- ☐
- ☐
- ☐
- ☐
- ☐
- ☐
- ☐
- ☐
- ☐
- ☐
- ☐

NOTES

February 2024

18 Sunday	19 Monday	20 Tuesday	21 Wednesday
☐	☐	☐	☐
☐	☐	☐	☐
☐	☐	☐	☐

NOTES

22
Thursday

☐ ....
☐ ....
☐ ....

23
Friday

☐ ....
☐ ....
☐ ....

24
Saturday

☐ ....
☐ ....
☐ ....

TOP TASKS

☐ ....
☐ ....
☐ ....
☐ ....
☐ ....
☐ ....
☐ ....
☐ ....
☐ ....
☐ ....
☐ ....
☐ ....
☐ ....
☐ ....
☐ ....
☐ ....
☐ ....
☐ ....
☐ ....
☐ ....
☐ ....

NOTES

March 2024

SUNDAY	MONDAY	TUESDAY	WEDNESDAY
3	4	5	6
10	11	12	13
17	18	19	20
24	25	26	27
31			

THURSDAY	FRIDAY	SATURDAY	Notes
	1	2	....
			....
			....
7	8	9	....
			....
14	15	16	....
			....
21	22	23	....
			....
28	29	30	....
			....

February 2024

25 Sunday	26 Monday	27 Tuesday	28 Wednesday
☐	☐	☐	☐
☐	☐	☐	☐
☐	☐	☐	☐

NOTES

29 Thursday	1 Friday	2 Saturday	TOP TASKS
☐	☐	☐	☐
☐	☐	☐	☐
☐	☐	☐	☐
			☐
			☐
			☐
			☐
			☐
			☐
			☐
			☐
			☐
			☐
			☐
			☐
			☐
			☐
			☐
			☐

NOTES

March 2024

3 Sunday	4 Monday	5 Tuesday	6 Wednesday
☐	☐	☐	☐
☐	☐	☐	☐
☐	☐	☐	☐

NOTES

7
Thursday

- ☐ ....
- ☐ ....
- ☐ ....

8
Friday

- ☐ ....
- ☐ ....
- ☐ ....

9
Saturday

- ☐ ....
- ☐ ....
- ☐ ....

TOP TASKS

- ☐
- ☐
- ☐
- ☐
- ☐
- ☐
- ☐
- ☐
- ☐
- ☐
- ☐
- ☐
- ☐
- ☐
- ☐
- ☐
- ☐
- ☐
- ☐
- ☐
- ☐

NOTES

10 Sunday	11 Monday	12 Tuesday	13 Wednesday
☐	☐	☐	☐ ....
☐	☐	☐	☐ ....
☐	☐	☐	☐ ....

NOTES

14 Thursday	15 Friday	16 Saturday	TOP TASKS
☐	☐	☐	☐
☐	☐	☐	☐
☐	☐	☐	☐
			☐
			☐
			☐
			☐
			☐
			☐
			☐
			☐
			☐
			☐
			☐
			☐
			☐
			☐
			☐
			☐
			☐

NOTES

March 2024

17 Sunday

- ☐ ....
- ☐ ....
- ☐ ....

18 Monday

- ☐ ....
- ☐ ....
- ☐ ....

19 Tuesday

- ☐ ....
- ☐ ....
- ☐ ....

20 Wednesday

- ☐ ....
- ☐ ....
- ☐ ....

NOTES

21 Thursday

- [ ] ....
- [ ] ....
- [ ] ....
- ....
- ....
- ....
- ....
- ....
- ....
- ....
- ....
- ....
- ....
- ....
- ....
- ....
- ....
- ....
- ....

22 Friday

- [ ] ....
- [ ] ....
- [ ] ....
- ....
- ....
- ....
- ....
- ....
- ....
- ....
- ....
- ....
- ....
- ....
- ....
- ....
- ....
- ....
- ....

23 Saturday

- [ ] ....
- [ ] ....
- [ ] ....
- ....
- ....
- ....
- ....
- ....
- ....
- ....
- ....
- ....
- ....
- ....
- ....
- ....
- ....
- ....
- ....

TOP TASKS

- [ ] ....
- [ ] ....
- [ ] ....
- [ ] ....
- [ ] ....
- [ ] ....
- [ ] ....
- [ ] ....
- [ ] ....
- [ ] ....
- [ ] ....
- [ ] ....
- [ ] ....
- [ ] ....
- [ ] ....
- [ ] ....
- [ ] ....
- [ ] ....
- [ ] ....
- [ ] ....

NOTES

24 Sunday	25 Monday	26 Tuesday	27 Wednesday
☐	☐	☐	☐
☐	☐	☐	☐
☐	☐	☐	☐

NOTES

28
Thursday

- [ ]
- [ ]
- [ ]

29
Friday

- [ ]
- [ ]
- [ ]

30
Saturday

- [ ]
- [ ]
- [ ]

TOP TASKS

- [ ]
- [ ]
- [ ]
- [ ]
- [ ]
- [ ]
- [ ]
- [ ]
- [ ]
- [ ]
- [ ]
- [ ]
- [ ]
- [ ]
- [ ]
- [ ]
- [ ]
- [ ]
- [ ]
- [ ]

NOTES

April 2024

SUNDAY	MONDAY	TUESDAY	WEDNESDAY
	1	2	3
7	8	9	10
14	15	16	17
21	22	23	24
28	29	30	

THURSDAY	FRIDAY	SATURDAY	Notes
4	5	6	....
			....
11	12	13	....
			....
18	19	20	....
			....
25	26	27	....
			....

March 2024

31 Sunday	1 Monday	2 Tuesday	3 Wednesday
☐	☐	☐	☐
☐	☐	☐	☐
☐	☐	☐	☐

NOTES

4 Thursday	5 Friday	6 Saturday	TOP TASKS
☐	☐	☐	☐
☐	☐	☐	☐
☐	☐	☐	☐
			☐
			☐
			☐
			☐
			☐
			☐
			☐
			☐
			☐
			☐
			☐
			☐
			☐
			☐
			☐
			☐
			☐

NOTES

April 2024

7 Sunday	8 Monday	9 Tuesday	10 Wednesday
☐	☐	☐	☐
☐	☐	☐	☐
☐	☐	☐	☐

NOTES

11 Thursday	12 Friday	13 Saturday	TOP TASKS
☐	☐	☐	☐
☐	☐	☐	☐
☐	☐	☐	☐
			☐
			☐
			☐
			☐
			☐
			☐
			☐
			☐
			☐
			☐
			☐
			☐
			☐
			☐
			☐
			☐

NOTES

April 2024

14 Sunday	15 Monday	16 Tuesday	17 Wednesday
☐	☐	☐	☐
☐	☐	☐	☐
☐	☐	☐	☐

NOTES

18
Thursday

- [ ]
- [ ]
- [ ]

19
Friday

- [ ]
- [ ]
- [ ]

20
Saturday

- [ ]
- [ ]
- [ ]

TOP TASKS

- [ ]
- [ ]
- [ ]
- [ ]
- [ ]
- [ ]
- [ ]
- [ ]
- [ ]
- [ ]
- [ ]
- [ ]
- [ ]
- [ ]
- [ ]
- [ ]
- [ ]
- [ ]
- [ ]
- [ ]

NOTES

April 2024

21 Sunday	22 Monday	23 Tuesday	24 Wednesday
☐	☐	☐	☐
☐	☐	☐	☐
☐	☐	☐	☐

NOTES

25
Thursday

☐ ....
☐ ....
☐ ....

26
Friday

☐ ....
☐ ....
☐ ....

27
Saturday

☐ ....
☐ ....
☐ ....

TOP TASKS

☐ ....
☐ ....
☐ ....
☐ ....
☐ ....
☐ ....
☐ ....
☐ ....
☐ ....
☐ ....
☐ ....
☐ ....
☐ ....
☐ ....
☐ ....
☐ ....
☐ ....
☐ ....
☐ ....
☐ ....

NOTES

May 2024

SUNDAY	MONDAY	TUESDAY	WEDNESDAY
			1
5	6	7	8
12	13	14	15
19	20	21	22
26	27	28	29

THURSDAY	FRIDAY	SATURDAY	Notes
2	3	4	....
			....
9	10	11	....
			....
16	17	18	....
			....
23	24	25	....
			....
30	31		....

April 2024

28 Sunday	29 Monday	30 Tuesday	1 Wednesday
☐	☐	☐	☐
☐	☐	☐	☐
☐	☐	☐	☐

NOTES

2 Thursday	3 Friday	4 Saturday	TOP TASKS
☐	☐	☐	☐
☐	☐	☐	☐
☐	☐	☐	☐
			☐
			☐
			☐
			☐
			☐
			☐
			☐
			☐
			☐
			☐
			☐
			☐
			☐
			☐
			☐
			☐
			☐

NOTES

May 2024

5 Sunday	6 Monday	7 Tuesday	8 Wednesday
☐	☐	☐	☐
☐	☐	☐	☐
☐	☐	☐	☐

NOTES

9 Thursday	10 Friday	11 Saturday	TOP TASKS
☐	☐	☐	☐
☐	☐	☐	☐
☐	☐	☐	☐
			☐
			☐
			☐
			☐
			☐
			☐
			☐
			☐
			☐
			☐
			☐
			☐
			☐
			☐
			☐
			☐
			☐

NOTES

May 2024

12 Sunday	13 Monday	14 Tuesday	15 Wednesday
☐	☐	☐	☐
☐	☐	☐	☐
☐	☐	☐	☐

NOTES

16 Thursday	17 Friday	18 Saturday	TOP TASKS
☐	☐	☐	☐
☐	☐	☐	☐
☐	☐	☐	☐
			☐
			☐
			☐
			☐
			☐
			☐
			☐
			☐
			☐
			☐
			☐
			☐
			☐
			☐
			☐
			☐
			☐

NOTES

May 2024

19
Sunday

- [ ] ....
- [ ] ....
- [ ] ....

20
Monday

- [ ] ....
- [ ] ....
- [ ] ....

21
Tuesday

- [ ] ....
- [ ] ....
- [ ] ....

22
Wednesday

- [ ] ....
- [ ] ....
- [ ] ....

NOTES

23
Thursday

☐
☐
☐

24
Friday

☐
☐
☐

25
Saturday

☐
☐
☐

TOP TASKS

☐
☐
☐
☐
☐
☐
☐
☐
☐
☐
☐
☐
☐
☐
☐
☐
☐
☐
☐
☐

NOTES

June 2024

SUNDAY	MONDAY	TUESDAY	WEDNESDAY
2	3	4	5
9	10	11	12
16	17	18	19
23	24	25	26
30			

THURSDAY	FRIDAY	SATURDAY	Notes
		1	....
			....
6	7	8	....
13	14	15	....
20	21	22	....
27	28	29	....

May 2024

26 Sunday	27 Monday	28 Tuesday	29 Wednesday
☐	☐	☐	☐
☐	☐	☐	☐
☐	☐	☐	☐

NOTES

30
Thursday

- [ ]
- [ ]
- [ ]

31
Friday

- [ ]
- [ ]
- [ ]

1
Saturday

- [ ]
- [ ]
- [ ]

TOP TASKS

- [ ]
- [ ]
- [ ]
- [ ]
- [ ]
- [ ]
- [ ]
- [ ]
- [ ]
- [ ]
- [ ]
- [ ]
- [ ]
- [ ]
- [ ]
- [ ]
- [ ]
- [ ]
- [ ]
- [ ]

NOTES

June 2024

2 Sunday	3 Monday	4 Tuesday	5 Wednesday
☐	☐	☐	☐
☐	☐	☐	☐
☐	☐	☐	☐

NOTES

6
Thursday

☐ ....
☐ ....
☐ ....

7
Friday

☐ ....
☐ ....
☐ ....

8
Saturday

☐ ....
☐ ....
☐ ....

TOP TASKS

☐ ....
☐ ....
☐ ....
☐ ....
☐ ....
☐ ....
☐ ....
☐ ....
☐ ....
☐ ....
☐ ....
☐ ....
☐ ....
☐ ....
☐ ....
☐ ....
☐ ....
☐ ....
☐ ....

NOTES

June 2024

9 Sunday	10 Monday	11 Tuesday	12 Wednesday
☐	☐	☐	☐
☐	☐	☐	☐
☐	☐	☐	☐

NOTES

13
Thursday

- ☐
- ☐
- ☐

14
Friday

- ☐
- ☐
- ☐

15
Saturday

- ☐
- ☐
- ☐

TOP TASKS

- ☐
- ☐
- ☐
- ☐
- ☐
- ☐
- ☐
- ☐
- ☐
- ☐
- ☐
- ☐
- ☐
- ☐
- ☐
- ☐
- ☐
- ☐
- ☐

NOTES

June 2024

16 Sunday	17 Monday	18 Tuesday	19 Wednesday
☐	☐	☐	☐
☐	☐	☐	☐
☐	☐	☐	☐

NOTES

20
Thursday

- [ ]
- [ ]
- [ ]

21
Friday

- [ ]
- [ ]
- [ ]

22
Saturday

- [ ]
- [ ]
- [ ]

TOP TASKS

- [ ]
- [ ]
- [ ]
- [ ]
- [ ]
- [ ]
- [ ]
- [ ]
- [ ]
- [ ]
- [ ]
- [ ]
- [ ]
- [ ]
- [ ]
- [ ]
- [ ]
- [ ]
- [ ]
- [ ]

NOTES

June 2024

23 Sunday
- ☐ ....
- ☐ ....
- ☐ ....

24 Monday
- ☐ ....
- ☐ ....
- ☐ ....

25 Tuesday
- ☐ ....
- ☐ ....
- ☐ ....

26 Wednesday
- ☐ ....
- ☐ ....
- ☐ ....

NOTES

27
Thursday

☐ ⋯⋯⋯⋯⋯⋯⋯⋯⋯⋯
☐ ⋯⋯⋯⋯⋯⋯⋯⋯⋯⋯
☐ ⋯⋯⋯⋯⋯⋯⋯⋯⋯⋯

28
Friday

☐ ⋯⋯⋯⋯⋯⋯⋯⋯⋯⋯
☐ ⋯⋯⋯⋯⋯⋯⋯⋯⋯⋯
☐ ⋯⋯⋯⋯⋯⋯⋯⋯⋯⋯

29
Saturday

☐ ⋯⋯⋯⋯⋯⋯⋯⋯⋯⋯
☐ ⋯⋯⋯⋯⋯⋯⋯⋯⋯⋯
☐ ⋯⋯⋯⋯⋯⋯⋯⋯⋯⋯

TOP TASKS

☐ ⋯⋯⋯⋯⋯⋯⋯⋯⋯⋯
☐ ⋯⋯⋯⋯⋯⋯⋯⋯⋯⋯
☐ ⋯⋯⋯⋯⋯⋯⋯⋯⋯⋯
☐ ⋯⋯⋯⋯⋯⋯⋯⋯⋯⋯
☐ ⋯⋯⋯⋯⋯⋯⋯⋯⋯⋯
☐ ⋯⋯⋯⋯⋯⋯⋯⋯⋯⋯
☐ ⋯⋯⋯⋯⋯⋯⋯⋯⋯⋯
☐ ⋯⋯⋯⋯⋯⋯⋯⋯⋯⋯
☐ ⋯⋯⋯⋯⋯⋯⋯⋯⋯⋯
☐ ⋯⋯⋯⋯⋯⋯⋯⋯⋯⋯
☐ ⋯⋯⋯⋯⋯⋯⋯⋯⋯⋯
☐ ⋯⋯⋯⋯⋯⋯⋯⋯⋯⋯
☐ ⋯⋯⋯⋯⋯⋯⋯⋯⋯⋯
☐ ⋯⋯⋯⋯⋯⋯⋯⋯⋯⋯
☐ ⋯⋯⋯⋯⋯⋯⋯⋯⋯⋯
☐ ⋯⋯⋯⋯⋯⋯⋯⋯⋯⋯
☐ ⋯⋯⋯⋯⋯⋯⋯⋯⋯⋯
☐ ⋯⋯⋯⋯⋯⋯⋯⋯⋯⋯
☐ ⋯⋯⋯⋯⋯⋯⋯⋯⋯⋯

NOTES

July 2024

SUNDAY	MONDAY	TUESDAY	WEDNESDAY
	1	2	3
7	8	9	10
14	15	16	17
21	22	23	24
28	29	30	31

THURSDAY	FRIDAY	SATURDAY	Notes
4	5	6	....
			....
11	12	13	....
			....
18	19	20	....
			....
25	26	27	....
			....

June 2024

30 Sunday	1 Monday	2 Tuesday	3 Wednesday
☐	☐	☐	☐ ....
☐	☐	☐	☐ ....
☐	☐	☐	☐ ....

NOTES

4 Thursday	5 Friday	6 Saturday	TOP TASKS
☐	☐	☐	☐
☐	☐	☐	☐
☐	☐	☐	☐
			☐
			☐
			☐
			☐
			☐
			☐
			☐
			☐
			☐
			☐
			☐
			☐
			☐
			☐
			☐
			☐

NOTES

July 2024

7 Sunday	8 Monday	9 Tuesday	10 Wednesday
☐	☐	☐	☐
☐	☐	☐	☐
☐	☐	☐	☐

NOTES

11 Thursday	12 Friday	13 Saturday	TOP TASKS
☐	☐	☐	☐
☐	☐	☐	☐
☐	☐	☐	☐
			☐
			☐
			☐
			☐
			☐
			☐
			☐
			☐
			☐
			☐
			☐
			☐
			☐
			☐
			☐

NOTES

July 2024

14 Sunday	15 Monday	16 Tuesday	17 Wednesday
☐	☐	☐	☐
☐	☐	☐	☐
☐	☐	☐	☐

NOTES

18
Thursday

- [ ]
- [ ]
- [ ]

19
Friday

- [ ]
- [ ]
- [ ]

20
Saturday

- [ ]
- [ ]
- [ ]

TOP TASKS

- [ ]
- [ ]
- [ ]
- [ ]
- [ ]
- [ ]
- [ ]
- [ ]
- [ ]
- [ ]
- [ ]
- [ ]
- [ ]
- [ ]
- [ ]
- [ ]
- [ ]
- [ ]
- [ ]
- [ ]

NOTES

July 2024

21 Sunday	22 Monday	23 Tuesday	24 Wednesday
☐	☐	☐	☐
☐	☐	☐	☐
☐	☐	☐	☐

NOTES

25
Thursday

☐ ....
☐ ....
☐ ....

26
Friday

☐ ....
☐ ....
☐ ....

27
Saturday

☐ ....
☐ ....
☐ ....

TOP TASKS

☐ ....
☐ ....
☐ ....
☐ ....
☐ ....
☐ ....
☐ ....
☐ ....
☐ ....
☐ ....
☐ ....
☐ ....
☐ ....
☐ ....
☐ ....
☐ ....
☐ ....
☐ ....
☐ ....
☐ ....

NOTES

July 2024

28 Sunday	29 Monday	30 Tuesday	31 Wednesday
☐	☐	☐	☐
☐	☐	☐	☐
☐	☐	☐	☐

NOTES

1
Thursday

☐ ....
☐ ....
☐ ....

2
Friday

☐ ....
☐ ....
☐ ....

3
Saturday

☐ ....
☐ ....
☐ ....

TOP TASKS

☐ ....
☐ ....
☐ ....
☐ ....
☐ ....
☐ ....
☐ ....
☐ ....
☐ ....
☐ ....
☐ ....
☐ ....
☐ ....
☐ ....
☐ ....
☐ ....
☐ ....
☐ ....
☐ ....

NOTES

Notes

Like Freebies?

EMAIL US: *PrintedBlissPlanners@gmail.com*

WRITE **"ACADEMIC 2023"** IN THE SUBJECT LINE.

WE WILL SEND YOU AN INSPIRING THANK YOU GIFT!

Printed in Great Britain
by Amazon

27452551R00077